Last Exposures

Also by Cathryn Hankla

POETRY

Phenomena (1983)

Afterimages (1991)

Negative History (1997)

Texas School Book Depository (2000)

Emerald City Blues (2002)

Poems for the Pardoned (2002)

FICTION

Learning the Mother Tongue (1987)

A Blue Moon in Poorwater (1988, reprint 1998)

The Land Between (2003)

Cathryn Hankla

LAST EXPOSURES

a sequence of poems

LOUISIANA STATE UNIVERSITY PRESS BATON ROUGE 2004

Manufactured in the United States of America
First printing

Designer: Laura Roubique Gleason
Typeface: Minion text, Engraver's Gothic display
Printer and binder: Thomson-Shore, Inc.

Library of Congress Cataloging-in-Publication Data:

Hankla, Cathryn, 1958–
Last exposures : a sequence of poems / Cathryn Hankla.
p. cm.
ISBN 0-0871-2947-X (alk. paper) — ISBN 0-8071-2948-8 (pbk. : alk. paper)
I. Title.
PS3558.A4689L37 2004
811'.54—dc22

2003015269

The paper in this book meets the guidelines for permanence and durability of the Committee on Production Guidelines for Book Longevity of the Council on Library Resources. ∞

The author wishes to thank Hollins University for a Cabell Fellowship and Foundacion Valparaiso for a residency, which provided time and space for the composition of many of these poems. The first three poems were inspired by Robert Gober's artwork, "Slides of a Changing Painting." The author also offers grateful acknowledgment to the editors of the following publications, in which some of the poems herein originally appeared, sometimes in a different form: *Appalachian Heritage:* "Only Thyme," "Killing the Snake on Summer's Cusp"; *Connecticut Review:* "Twenty-Five Minute Exposure, II"; *Exquisite Corpse:* "There's a Hole in the Man's Chest, but the Man Is Living," "Sometimes the Man Turns into a Woman," "Abstraction from a Life in the Body," "Immanent Creation," "When Leaving, no Reentry Permitted"; *Oxford Magazine:* "Wind River Canyon"; *Passages North:* "Not Having Read *The Poetics of Space.*"

"Encounter," *Common Wealth: Contemporary Poets of Virginia,* ed. R.T. Smith and Sarah Kennedy, University Press of Virginia, 2003.

"Ghost Family," and "How to Stop a Camel," *Cabin Fever: Poets at Joaquin Miller's Cabin, 1984–2001,* ed. Jacklyn W. Potter et al., Word Works, Inc., 2003.

Contents

Last Exposures

There's a Hole in the Man's Chest, but the Man Is Living

Branches transform to a man's shoulders,
The space between becomes his trunk.

How much that we know of men is really about trees?

Their chests grow bark.
The knot holes of their emotions
Sometimes rot or hold disease.

Heartwood can hollow from within,
And roots seek water in a dry pile of rocks.

Mushrooms steal away the rain meant
To nurture leaves. Silent fungus, invisible, ubiquitous,
A subterranean web growing larger

Than a man or a forest.

Sometimes the Man Turns into a Woman

Sometimes lines beneath the nipples deepen,
The thatch of hair disappears,
And I think I see breasts.

But the 3-D hole remains.

The injury could be self-inflicted.
It could bloom flowers, but it never does.
When I try to look through it, the hole descends,

Tripling in depth, just when I think I spy its end.

Abstraction from a Life in the Body

Any body can turn into a painted landscape
Or a page in a book. Flat planes are always
Ready to erase our dimensions,

As when we write half a truth and call it fiction.
The amount unknown, the vast interior,
Molten core and a million facts—

The man is lying on his back in a hospital bed.
Hourly, the x-ray machine hovers over his chest.
Soon the sheet will cover his head.

For now, he is breathing.
For now, I call him "Father."
In a few days his hand

Will draw away, his eyes will dull
On a point I cannot follow.

Not Having Read *The Poetics of Space*

The pilfered nest rests easily on the palm,
Open to air, chicks departed.
Late summer, I remove it from the floodlight,

Arrange it on the ground,
In an elbow of weathered wood.
I save the mud-crusted hollow, the divining

Twigs, stems, moss that were pressed to the breast
Curve of a Carolina wren. The bird's instinct
Will not return it to this twining—

Snow may fill this clever bowl—
Yet I have an instinct to preserve its story,
Written wisps of down, written sticks,

Bit of ribbon where hatchlings pecked through
Rough shell, and somehow flew.

San Francisco in the Background

Traffic rumbles, occasionally emits a squawk,
A siren recedes, doves coo, chatter resumes
In several tongues questing direction.

Someone's daughter or mother boards
The bus with an aid dog and announces,
"That Chinese food gives me gas, does it you?"

For my mother, memory is stronger than the moment,
Deeper than San Francisco Bay, which we are told
Rivals the Grand Canyon.

Nearly sixty years ago, a war
Pulled her west to attend my father.
He was not my father then,

But a naval officer. Their life together
Remains a mystery to me.
A man sits down beside my mother

Taking more space than his share.
She balances and grips her purse,
The bus jostles her and lurches.

I try to reassure her across the aisle.
She has trouble with one ear,
Smiles and nods as if agreeing,

But I know she hasn't heard a word.

20/20

The woman's flat chest has thickened
With the muscle of sweat work,
But it is two-dimensional,

A background to a well-defined hole.
As with a cave that opens through rock,
The light gradually recedes.

A long time ago an attractive opening appeared
And swallowed a pair of long-stemmed roses.
I stuck my head in to see where they went,

Thinking it was the heart's place they occupied,
That the heart had bloomed.
There was nothing inside

But a darkness beyond comprehension,
A fearful child who never learned
Whose child she was.

No one's fault and everyone's failing.
Scar tissue clogs
The cavern leading to her heart.

Life on the Rocks

The mineral green of desiccated seas
Spills down low hills, a mirage of grass
In an ocher-red realm. In Wyoming,

Time-compressed bones can oxidize
With one breath of fresh air and literally
Vanish. Trexler, the paleontologist, wraps

Each stony find in a plaster cast, to remove
It to the lab. Cocooned, perhaps, for years,
The relics await a fine chisel's tapping

That will map surfaces of vertebra, tibia,
Pelvis, or skull. Sometimes teeth marks
Reveal a territory battle millenniums old.

My father wanted pumice from Iceland.
The 1958 Encyclopaedia Britannica
Proclaimed the powder a natural island

Product. To fulfill one request in a lifetime
Of few expressions, I roamed
Every chemist shop

For black magic in a jar, and found
Only a chunk of porous, volcanic
Rock stolen from a black sand beach,

Which I carried to drop into my father's hand.
I told him that they must not make
It nowadays. "Not making any more rocks?"

He laughed. Five months later,
The pocked stone sat in my living room.
We buried him next to his mother.

Carnoy's Solution

The yellowed 3x5 note
Still holds typed words:
    Abs. Alcohol 30

    Chloroform 15
    Glacial Acetic Ac 5
    Ferric Chloride 5.

A lone period chases the last five, as written above.
A cure for something goes unheeded,
An obsolete solution

Haunts my file. My father's
Recipe is clear and yet not clear.
His chemistry portends

For me no recognizable compound,
Only a wounding of necessity,
The obscurity

Of innocent intent
So long ago rendered—
Stacked, filed, forgotten—

Until my mother the resurrectionist
Slaps the card upon my palm.
I drive away from her through an insect swarm

Of rain that imitates suns spun from a mirror ball,
Radiating around the car
As if I were drunk on a dance floor,

As if I were anywhere and anyone
But here, alone, on a dark road, with no solutions,
With only my own light to steer by.

Stop at Lust

On the billboard, the last letter of the town
Has been vandalized from K to T,
Population 100, Elevation 8,000 feet.

I keep driving, fooling no one
With the momentum of my mistake.
The landscape stretches to hold expansive

Imperatives—it's a place where
Lust shifts easily into Lost. And from Lost
It's a stone's throw to Last Chance.

Following FedEx from Shoshoni
To Casper, I see the piercing sunburst
Of daisy dancers edging high desert scrub.

Moneta, population 10. Hiland, population 10.
I wonder if it's even more
Difficult to find a date out here

Than where I'm from, an area of over 100,000—
Almost a quarter of this whole state
Or half the population of Iceland,

Yet I see houses and children, sidewalks,
And roaming pets. Happiness
Lurking everywhere, happiness on the lam.

Sundance

Anointed braves bore
The weight of bison skulls lashed
With leather thongs, fastened

To pegs beneath their breasts.
Discouraged by missionaries,
The summer ritual's meaning

Has gone the way of Brontosaurus.
A construct like the Jackalope
Or Frankenstein's monster,

"Thunder lizard" bore the head
Of the wrong animal for a hundred years.
Try wearing a hat that doesn't fit

For even half a day. Camarasaurus's
Skull perched on the wrong body
Because O. C. Marsh's party didn't figure

On the drift of bones, bones sifting
Layers to collect
In bone beds, a scramble of eons.

The rock that yields dinosaurs
Is also called *Sundance.* Factual
Apatosaurus replaces a chimera.

Wind River Canyon

I lower my speed for the blasted holes,
Bored tunnels speckling
The wound route of Wind River.

I rein in my power, my mind from morbid
Possibilities that have already occurred—
My father's missing a curve,

Flipping his car like a turtle.
Revived on the roadside, yet broken
Beyond belief. Shunted skull

And every rib ruptured. Bruised like old
Elephant hide, my mother said, shaking
Her head before the fact.

Cambrian, Precambrian—rock rolls by.
What's the difference of a few million years?

The Only Rabbit in Wyoming

We are familiar with elk, with lizard,
Turtle creation panels, and buffalo,
But this rabbit's cultural area is in New Mexico.

Which begs the question of travel.
Through time and space
Along back roads, following a faded map,

A key jingling on the dash, I weave
Open range, dodge creatures on the hoof,
To unlock the green gate

Leading to Legend Rock. At first I scramble
The wrong knoll, skittish as the rattler
I fear. I've tracked pictographs in The Maze

Of Utah on a far hotter one than this,
Boxed in a canyon with a mountain lion
Pacing a ledge above my foolish head,

But something today crawls over my skin.
I scatter loose dirt, climb
With a knocking in my chest.

I don't know if time or space, or loss
Has brought me here
To crumbling, vulnerable cliffs,

Zoomorphs and anthropomorphs
Etched in a vanished tongue
That may yet conjure.

The Laughing Man

Doted on Friday, his poodle.
A family favorite, youngest of six,
He remained close to his mother.

Crowning the chapel aisle
The open casket discloses
Danny's broad, gray face,

Whose chest caught gunfire
Because he was gay.
An act "nonsensical," some will say,

Of the "deranged drifter,"
And "inexplicable." Another
Victim cries above the laughing man,

Her left hand bandaged in pale salute.
"I'm sorry," she says. "So sorry about this."
The scars of five others, of a town will heal

Far more slowly than one might think,
As the coverage dies down
And people go about their grief

For a world no one has ever seen—
For the right to love
The laughing man.

in memory of Danny Lee Overstreet, 1957–2000

Laramie, or Our Town

Outside of Laramie,
Matthew Shepard was hitched to a post
And beaten. He had a sweet

Disposition, which saved him
No trouble and spared
Him nothing, not even

His life. Two rowdies thought
They'd get away with murder
By pointing the finger.

I stretch my legs around quiet blocks,
Through a neighborhood where
Children roam freely home

From school. In the next generation,
In the dead night of any town,
Will the owl hoot a different cry

And the moon look down
On a world gone to sleep
And finally awakened?

Rivers

Of what
Arroyos on Mars might mean,
Scientists are trained

Not to be sure.
When a man's chest tightens
Then pours rivulets from

A wound, we know what we see.
And yet the reasons remain
Obscure. A man might have

Drunk too much in the afternoon,
Only to awaken in a hospital room
With chest tubes and rattling breath.

A man might have gone
To a bar after work, embraced
A friend and been targeted

By an unstable vet, who, without
Employment or home
Was still able to buy a gun.

Never turn your back to the door.
Never take off your boots or
Your spurs.

Ever wonder if there's water on Mars?

Anniversary

After a year I read his name on a brass placard.
There has been no rush in the manufacture.
As everyone knows, the dead

Can wait. High on this hill
Above the railroad tracks and the pharmacy
(Where Dr. Pepper concocted his soft drink,

Containing a secret dash of prune juice),
The marble foot stone has been set.
Veteran of two wars, the official brass tells us,

Yet it's incorrect—
Or maybe not. The long war after the war
Should count as well. Years of shadow boxing

In the basement, fire storms of emotion
That left us all shell-shocked. The final rush
Of his wheels, his tumbling into air

And collapsed lung's gasp.
If I had known him better, I could better judge
His patience or impatience with human error.

Lost Diamond

He's not buried with the diamond
And it's nowhere to be found.
After several years lost,

Lying fallow, it ploughed up
With red clay for the new sewer line.
How many chances can one

Man command? He survived
World War II, in a small support carrier
Whose wooden decks held a hundred

Definitive ways to meet a fiery death,
By landing accident, torpedo, kamikazes
Appearing out of smoke and heaven.

He made it through the famous Battle
Of Leyte Gulf, when his fleet was
Written off, stood watching as a nearby

Baby flattop succumbed and sailors
Leapt into the sea. Wondering, why
Not me? Wondering, over the years,

Why his brother lost his youngest,
His wife, and finally his own life to cancer.
Wondering as his parents died

And his sister, leaving him alone to bear
The family name. "Things turn
Out as they're supposed to," he told me,

From his hospital bed, thinking he
Might beat the odds one last time—
Or maybe not. Maybe it was I who held on

To that thought, as I dream now of finding
The diamond ring, miraculously
Recovered, but lost again.

Oil of Smoke

"Oil of Smoke" sits on the back shelf,
Label scratched and crumbling,
Not snake oil, but a potent distillation

Passed through wood smoke like ham.
Edgar Cayce speaks from his trance, directing
The elder pharmacist to procure the last bottle.

A boy's stubborn sore, treated with the balm,
Heals with no scar. As I watch,
My father's bruised-black skin,

Brain lesion, broken ribs, bloody
Chest tubes, and catheter appear to improve.
His swelling deflates. The illusion holds until

The doctors move him to Progressive Care,
Where he is tortured by his roommate's ginger ale,
Coffee, and ice cream, starved even of water.

His throat, finally tube free, refuses
To swallow. It's only a matter
Of a germ, droplets lodging in weakened lungs,

Then of a short time before we gather.
Across the road, into traffic,
A little girl runs, unaware.

A pickup skids sideways out of a curve. Cars
Screech, scorching rubber to a halt. And the girl—
Keeps running to the other side.

Encounter

Out of dusky silence and staggering
Time, from a swollen afternoon
Of elevated leg and painkillers,

Comes the car and driver. If thoughts
Briefly divert, their range is narrow:
Bucks in rut routinely damage vehicles

Along this stretch. The shoulders
Are carefully scanned. Her father
Wrecked last week and may not recover.

The driver, doubly chastened, still doesn't see
A black angus leveraging for broke,
Head bowed to barbed wire, munching

With backside and all fours planted
In the road. It's over almost before
It begins: red car bounces into oncoming lane,

Radiator leaks fluorescent green,
Black angus veers off its hooves, releasing
Anguished groans. Its orange-tagged ear

Writhes and slumps. The driver stumbles
From her car into the shadowed weeds,
Alone. Wind chills her to the bone.

Encircled

A full moon's form appears
As a disk, not a sphere. After dark,
We hear a cry and cannot trace

Sound to source. Nothing is seen,
Only appears. All we do is look
Into the darkness, seeing flattened

Dimensions, tempted to believe
We are keen. Yet what might answer
From hidden, multiple points

Were we able to sense more than see?
Something telling us to swerve,
Something tugging us back

To a house on a high hill rattled by weather,
Into unheated rooms where voices began,
To a shore that issues always toward

A father or mother we miss but never knew.
Salt water returns and returns,
Tides are meant to rive the sand.

Immanent Creation

Standing over the graves of van Gogh
And his brother, I felt a vague stirring, as of
A journey commencing from Auvers-sur-Oise.

I then walked the surround of yellow fields
Brushstrokes have illumined. Art takes a life-
Time, gathers from the living, yet returns

Far more than reflection. There may be
No other way than this to live, risking
Nothingness. In the background, in the corner

Of a rustic bedroom draped in blue, inside
A sound, within a color transformed by
Lucidity and the sheen of varnish,

What is it that you can see?

When Leaving, No Reentry Permitted

Un billet, a ticket, marked no return.
Here wander, inhaling scents of lush
Pink blooms. Drooping and dripping

From quick snips, invisible trusses.
It is almost too much, this plot snug
As a suburban yard, a verdurous

Palette. Wander trodden paths,
Heady with deep cultivation. The pace
Sweeps along to the ponds. Don't glance

Back to the charming abode. Each
Leather chair bears the impression
Of a wide, famous behind,

The impression that this painter
Has just stepped out for an extra loaf
Or a plein air sketch.

Alas, without proper credentials,
Claude Monet cannot rejoin us:
Toute sortie du Musée est definitive.

Last Exposures

After more than a year,
My mother hands me his camera
Straight from its case.

I move outside to photograph
The paint job, drips and daubs
Left by a sloppy hand,

Evidence of the widow's lot:
Targeted for shoddy work.
Even her car wheel was ripped off.

I shoot the remaining three frames,
Go back inside to rewind,
Reload. The canister plops

Into my hand, his last exposures.
I try to imagine them
At the far end of the banal—

Whales blowing breath from the depths,
Molten whorls inside the moon—
Afraid to see what he's left us.

Home Movies

From the basement, a mold-crusted
Projector and ten metal
Canisters emerge. Silent home movies

Shot when more light was required,
And the memories we made had to take place
In the open on sunny days.

We remember the beach, the bent
Serving spoon scooping sand,
Glinting now its natural silver,

Better preserved than flesh that flickers
Black and white, assuming a gray
Tone of regret. Three minutes of little girls

Dancing in tutus across the lawn.
Then a clip of soldiers on leave, sporting leis,
Hawaiian shirts. They stand facing

The photographer, not opening
Their mouths or moving. This is not
A still, but it's hard to tell the difference.

"Where is that?" we ask over and over.
And not recognizing our father, "Who are
Those men?" The refrain repeats without our

Comprehension. "That was the war.
Now, it's bedtime." We leave our father
Flicking ashes in a darkened room.

Images of a Golf Match

Ghostly golfers in a season out of time
Find sudden death on a fairway in Maui
Or California. Pinehurst maybe.

The blurry swaths of green framed
By the TV set could be of any tournament,
And yet a few clues remain:

Bare legs signal the presence of women,
But not just any. This is a rare
Event in which top players are paired.

In one photo, a woman reverences a putt.
Another shot reveals a male profile washed free
Of any particular identity.

I wanted my father's memory lapses
To be filled in, sharpened, as I want these
Images found in his camera to be clear.

TV news blared above his hospital bed.
His eyes registered a flickering shock
When I said, "Payne Stewart is dead.

His plane crashed. It lost compression."
"I'm a wreck," my father replied,
In a voice raspy from ventilation.

Hummingbird

While you were not talking to me,
I cruised to Italy
And lived in Japan on the snowy isle

Of Hokkaido for a year.
The following, I applied
Myself to the study

Of the pseudoscience of the inner ear
And won a contest
Of wills. While you refused

To countenance a conversation,
I plied my dog with questions,
Asking him where the path

Of least resistance had fled,
Where the antiseptic tang
Of Becherovka over ice?

I asked if he remembered
Once having seen his own face
In a mirror. While you were

In your time of fretting,
I called your parents to report you
(Just kidding).

I drank out of a plastic cup,
Pretending it was a party. I joined a cult
Of devotées who worshipped me.

Across the grass just growing,
I watched for my dead father's shadow.
And although

We were not in its proper season,
And I knew it,
I waited for the hummingbird.

Gossip at the PO

If it were my house
I wouldn't build so close to the road.
You should see that woman's

Collection of hats, my lord! One tilts
Like a windmill, the other's some kind
Of dirty white fur. The chow

Got run over but only crushed one
Paw. I took it in, my little baby.
Have you noticed the burros?

Excuse me, but is this key
Supposed to work my lock?
Let me help you. One time

The wind was blowing so hard
When I opened the outside letter box
That I lost a piece or two.

I hope it wasn't one of your bills.
My back aches like teeth.
I wear magnets to bed and under my feet.

That girl who had the baby?
Her husband left. And
That carrier who disappeared, she never

Showed up with our mail.
She had a restraining order—
But the louse kidnapped her in a van.

I was just talking to her last week.
She let down her guard.
Did you hear about what happened

Over at Newport Road? The bus driver
Saw a guy parked near her stop.
Something didn't set right with her,

So she let the kids off farther down,
You never know about people,
And watched them to their doors.

The next day he was in the paper,
Blew himself away with a rifle.
You just never know.

A Fragment of the Author's Manuscript in Her Own Hand

I took my grief into Old Brompton Street
Where a deer hock was carved
In a restaurant window by a waiter dressed in black.

BBC reports 200,000 cullings
Of Cambrian sheep, carcass pyres curling
Smoke into the night.

I followed my shadow into whitewashed
Rooms of cutting edge art, halted before
Serrano's framed morgue

To discern rat poison results from drowned,
Mottled flesh, irreparable burns.
I know no English for my condition, nor

Words for the querulous expression
Of my dad, dead at 80 in a hospital bed—
The constant furrow given by the mortician

To his brow. All day I am silent, surrounded,
Alone. It grows cold,
My socks soggy. Walking past the wrecks

Of Aldgate East to Whitechapel Gallery,
My gaze befalls a man selling guides
Who chills me with the word, "Alien."

I want to push my head between "Heaven
And Earth," Viola's twin video screens locked
In tête-à-tête, so close as to be kissing:

The artist's mother lies dying above
His newborn son's first expressions, none
Of them fearful. I know I am neither

Here nor there, in fugitive colors,
More fragile than ever.

A Fragment of the Author's Manuscript in Her Own Hand, II

In the final circle, at the end of Hell,
Dante climbed the hairy left leg
Of the old monster himself,

Against gravity, lost in the short locks
Of the torso, disoriented as the master
Botticelli must have been—

Fifteen years (1480–95) he pored over
Sheep's vellum, with metal stylus
Gripped, then inked those grooves,

Making visible delicate circle and year.
Hell wore thin as the master's
Hair, though more detailed than Paradise,

Which piddled out in a splash of light.
Blank pages torn from a hidden book—
No one bad and no one good.

Rooster Loco

The crazy rooster of Mojácar has been crowing
For centuries. Some say the bird was abandoned near
Mojácar Vieja in a fit of Moorish

Bad humor back in 1100 B.C.E. Ever since,
It has been screaming. Around its neck,
Like a Hollywood producer, it wears

A megaphone. And when the rooster
Raises that flare to its dry little lips
That before only pecked the husks of kernels,

The mealy grubs of the desert,
There is no one sleeping in Mojácar Playa.
And in the village, forget it.

Only the rooster can dream.
On Viernes Santo the rooster loco dons sunglasses
And is carried aloft by men dressed in black suits.

Their white gloves lift him along uneven,
Twisting streets. A virgin on crutches sings an aria
From a balcony as the rooster

Dips around the final bend in the street,
Floating down to the site of the first city gates.
No one can see the gates, only rumors.

There, a marching band of clarinets,
Tubas, and one snare drum
Plays Dixie Swing, while the old women

Of Mojácar, the ones who can remember
When there was no rooster, cry mournful tears.
The rooster loves all of the attention, let me tell you,

Especially the virgin in blue jeans who pops
A button on her blouse when she sings.
And afterwards, when the rooster receives churros

From the priest. Oh, what a crowing!
Everyone licks sugar and grease from bright fingers
And sips café con leche, while the butcher

Sharpens his knife for the hen.

Upon Waking

There's going to be something you're lacking
And something you give.
There's sometimes a crease in your face

Upon waking. That's how it is.
When you walk the road into town, two greyhounds
Snooze on a giant mound of mulch.

One raises its head as you near the bend
And slowly lowers it again as you march on.
The mountain is always there in the back of your mind,

Behind the house that really is a world.
Behind the mountain, what is there to know?
Each afternoon the wind makes a changeling of the weather,

Tosses sheets and shirts and socks in more directions
Than four. Each night another shadow forms
On a different side of the mountain that is always

Shifting in your mind. You peek between the pages
Of books, looking
Sometimes between the open buttons of a blouse.

You walk the road, you return. The phone rings
And you answer to a different tongue. The world comes
Through the window like a flat photograph of the sun.

The sun falls down at your feet.
The mountain knows your name, every one.
There is a love always ending and a love just begun.

When you look down on the roof from the town,
You see where you began. When you look back to
Your country of origin, where language

First formed, there is nothing there and everything.
You live outside of words and live for words.
The tongues are running over you like the wind.

Your face is as familiar as the moon on a clear morning.
In your country, how do you say it?
In mine we say, *Hello, give me your hand.*

Other Rooms

In another room, he rises and shakes out his shoes.
He hopes for yet dreads the scorpions
Nesting in dark folds of dreams.

Each morning a new fear unfolds: maybe
The scant water will run purple or his earwax sprout
Like corn. The window might burn an image

Of the sun into his computer. If he walks too slowly
His belly will grow, too fast and the women cannot
Follow. Everything a dilemma, but to everyone

He must divulge. In his knapsack, there's
A jester wrapped up like a jacket, waiting
For inclement weather. It has a hood of course.

Sparrows leave pills of shit on his terrace.
News from home reads like a roman à clef:
In Chapter One, an actor kills himself. In Two,

The leading man is stabbed in a disco by a fan.
Bad blood like a faucet dripping on and on,
As predictable as the phone finally making its purr.

In Lorca, a procession of hooded figures winds
The street like el río, and on the crowded banks
Spectators point at gold brocade,

At horses and white cone heads extending skyward
Minus eyes to guide them. It is seldom a problem.
In this darkness, all vision grows inwardly large.

His back sprouts antennae-like wings.
His hands, which before fumbled like flags
In stiff wind, now know a stone's lineage

Just by its heft in his palm. Not one
Of his amigos misses a fly with the swatter,
Or remembers his hometown.

for Robert Fass

Las Meninas (The Group)

"Here we should recall Picasso's fascination for open doors, windows and mirrors which he used to tackle perspective. Sometimes, as here, the opening is preceeded *[sic]* by the shadow of a human figure, sometimes not."

—English Guide to the *Museu Picasso de Barcelona*

Fling open the windows, show Velázquez
The door. The sun
Is knocking, and light, while only 20%

Of reality, is all that we can see. For me
Light is enough. Even color too much—pare
Down the decoration, slice the pear

To the mute seed, to monochrome. Sing
One note *loud,* leave off
The adverbial suffix. Just this once, she

Said, this encounter is on me. Any problems,
See me, not your head trip.
Here, you can travel without guilt.

Just touch, she said. Still, I wondered,
If anything were free after thirty.
Can 20% really be enough?

His ebony back stopped my heart, his muscles
Strung between shoulder blades and buttocks
Like music. The series goes on and on,

Variations on a group that is seldom repeating.
Men and women wear each other's skins
Like blankets against chill wind

And discard them in the sun.
Does no one ever say, *I will always,*
You are mine, you, my one?

Five Minute Exposure, Large Format

The moon comes up like an almond
And down like an orange.
It wasn't the moon, but the mountain.

The moonfish has a face that ends
In a healing. Your hands pass
Over the gash and all at once

There is singing. At thirty-five,
I was laid out by an excommunicated priest.
His hands felt like a firewalk

On a hot afternoon. The priest
Was a drunkard, but what did it matter?
The face of the moonfish

Slashes through the sky. The clouds open,
The light dances, angling in from the playa.
No one knows where the shadows

Come from. It's a mystery, like the hands
Of the priest, like the almonds that slip
From the blood orange of the night.

When his hands touched my forehead
I fell to the floor. I had asked to feel
What my lover felt—she who was

Opened by a surgeon's knife,
By the touch of a rapist when only
A child. Why should I feel what she

Wished to forget? I asked to know empathy.
I fell into a swoon and landed curled
On the floor. When she woke

From anesthesia, I gently stroked her
Forehead. The first words she spoke
Were "No, please don't."

Twenty-Five Minute Exposure

When you seek the mountain, you will reap
Something different. What did my mother
Always say? Well, she should have said

Something. Silence is never binding.
In Casa Mila the walls curve backwards.
Don't try to picture it. Slants depend upon

Your vantage point. We imagine ourselves
Always at the center. That is our problem.
Why do Americans have such big

Refrigerators? I cannot say for sure.
I picture the grocery store, which is always
Too bright, the vegetables oiled and sprayed

On schedule. There is something about
Saving, leftover from the depression
(My mother-in-law liked to tell the story

Of how her family, back on the farm,
Kept them alive in the city in the 1930s
With canned goods and sausage),

And there is something about profusion,
Its opposite.
When you think of America, do you see a map

Of Canada and Mexico, Central and South,
Or just the states? I try to say *Estados Unidos.*
I try to sound dignified about my profusion.

Did you know that in my country,
There are more children and women starving
Than anyone else? Did you know that

Domestic violence is the numero uno
Cause of death for women? More common
To be hurt by your man than by strangers.

How many rooms do you have in your house?
I lost five when I divorced,
Gained five with resettlement. The rooms

Are smaller now, too, but they come at a lower
Price. I have a neighbor who hates
Gays and women and is dangerous to dogs

And horses. One evening I drove past his hovel
To find him burning leaves in the road,
So close to his rotting front porch

As to be lethal. And inside the house? Three
Generations of children were sleeping.
This man once left a threatening

Message. His daughters have children
But no husbands. Is this something you
Picture when you think about my house?

Outside my window is a mountain I watch
For signs. In summer I only see its summit,
But in winter it sneaks into my hallway,

Steals into my bed. How could you turn
Down the mountain, I ask you? It's easier to know
Future than past. The present echoes like a drum.

Twenty-Five Minute Exposure, II

Stabs of stars rotate slowly over the flat
Height of Mojácar Vieja.
The light slats might spin faster if someone

Took a corner of the sky and flung
It like a top to tumble through
The Milky Way. No one does this.

At the summit, even a lone dog can
Discover the strange cistern that hovers
Within the solid mountain.

Ghosts and water collect in this font
And siphon to the core of the world,
Reappearing as smears of silent

Music in the sky. Green vines
Wind up the cool cement sides
Of this basin. Shadows conceal

Formulas carved in its belly.
There is a woman who captures the view
Through polished glass. Each night

She focuses on scars and specks, clawed
Coronas like tinctures released. She reveals
The scent of her darkness, the mountain,

By cloaking herself with her fears.
The night is a dangerous place
Only when you resist its embrace.

for Claudia Terstappen

Twenty Minute Exposure

The risen mountain, a block of polished iron.
Think of an iron after the fire is gone,
Its pyramid cooling on the silver

Board. What it meant to be a woman, a wife,
I watched my mother to learn. What I
Was taught: iron the underwear, after sprinkling

It from a bottle. Iron the handkerchiefs.
This is the article I was taught first to iron,
Not a shirt. With handkerchiefs, a little girl's

Mistakes don't matter. The square is folded
And placed in your father's back pocket.
Why do men use only cloth to blow

And women use paper? What I learned:
The invisible work of women, the wrinkles
On their faces. I learned that women can spend

Their lives making the world a better place for men.

Twenty Minute Exposure, II

I am sorry in many languages
Means you sacrifice a cow or maybe a pig.
Then, either way, you dress it with garlic.

My father fought Japanese, not Germans.
It was two wars, they say, and both
Are over. Tell me what we have learned

About endings. Tell me why certain pairs
Of hands hinge like wings at the thumb,
As if sculpted. Why certain eyes train

Toward the sun and retain bits of its fire,
Solid, like ore, but liquid, agua potable.
And, as she said, "like champagne."

If I should be someone else, thinking
Something else, tell me. This
Moment says there are no accidents,

Only fate. We are too old for grieving.
From downstairs, a German word
Curls up the stairs. Someone closes lips

And blows a kiss. I can hear it
Even though I am a *stupid American,*
The first phrase I learn in any language.

For all nations, is it the same?
A pendulum
Swings: we know what it means.

Firewalk

In La Rambla Granatilla south of Mojácar
Mica glitters beneath your feet.
Everything you have been taught

Falls away, echoing.
Monolithic, multicolored walls stretch
To form a canyon

Opening to the sea. Where have you
Been
That loneliness cannot follow, where

Thoughts cannot strike flint against your heart?
A ship edges over
Glassy waves. Strange green pods

Dangle alongside filmy leaves.
From the bushes, you hear
The liquid clicks of a shutter.

A trick with a rock we are trying to learn:
Cover the hand
With a round stone then rest another's palm

On top. In between, the rock holds steady,
The worlds of origin recede
For a long moment and anything is possible.

You choose to rub the iridescence
Between your palms, staining
Your grip with the juice of the sun.

Your hands shimmer like fishes, swimming
Ashore or walking toward the horizon.
The chirp of the gray and yellow tit pauses,

Then the shutter clicks. You turn your
Head and see la rambla on fire, the sun
Hammering sparks just before it dies.

Shadow

Language shadows your face
Like a charming hat
Like shoes over hot pavement

Language precedes and follows
Your movements, creeping
Over every landscape

Harboring the sun
You jingle it like keys
In your pocket, choosing

One word that will fit
The lock of his ear
The lock of her mouth

Words travel like water
And tumble like rocks
The words you say

The words you cannot

Quartz, La Loma

Sleeping or waking
Rivulets appear in the land,
Challenges that disturb

A way of thinking,
Seams of translucent
Quartz split a buff background.

Loose soil breaks
Open and your soles sink
To the ankle, past the knee,

To the crux of reason.
At sundown you wind
Through the canyon like a clock.

In the church tower
Bags of sand swing lower
On their ropes with each tock.

You push open a door
And you enter
Without stopping for permission.

A dry riverbed empties at the base
Of jutting shapes
That answer and listen

Forming an expression
That some might call a question.
A rock fits into the hand,

A hand fits into a pocket
Like a word in the socket
Where a tooth was pulled.

A bracelet circles your wrist,
Sleeping or waking,
No end and no beginning.

Killing the Snake on Summer's Cusp

A thin, spotted teenager—still, the copperhead's
Snub nose cannot be mistaken. I look
For the hoe but find only a cracked bat meant

For human invaders. I strike before the snake
Rounds the corner behind the dog's
Water bowl. I smash its head to the dirt.

Reflex bunches and writhes not knowing
That death has claimed it. The dog skitters,
Wondering what I'll do next.

Then I remember, it's the year of the snake.
I fear I have killed off all possibility.
The Möbius strip coils around a stick, grips

And bends back before I fling life and death
Into the branches beyond the fenced-in world
I pretend holds back the beasts.

Only Thyme

I pull you out by the roots, fierce love,
But you still smell of thyme and lemon.
What were you thinking, to die

Instead of wintering, after so many seasons
Of spring shoots and new greening?
Surely your gnarled, woody fibers

Are more alive than they look.
Yet after patient weeks of rain, nothing
Grows except the cutting I potted,

A woolly patch dwarfed by purple basil.
Making space for new plants, I pull up
Withered stems, baring your roots, and

The scent runs through me, like music
Pouring through a sieve
Of consciousness, leaving only this.

Trouble with Angels

Broken wing, broken when the phone rang
And a voice denied the obvious.
The cord stretched

Far enough to touch off a terra cotta explosion.
"Gotta go," I said
And glue the wing back on, I thought,

The one clipped when the doctor . . .
And time flew backwards. Only time,
Though, not consciousness.

I'm having trouble with angels.
This little one gets in the way
When I wash large pots and pans.

And this other one rises behind the stove eyes,
An extra pair.
Another at the top of the cabinet. Which

Of my selves mounted it there? I'm having
Trouble with angels watching over me
Too closely, trouble with too many souls

Looking for landing pads.
A hummingbird pair finds solace
At the top of the Jack Oak,

Encircles the house with fluttering too fast
To see. Look at this heart, pared open in my hand,
You Jack Ass, whom I loved better than you love

Your golden parachute. But I've only
Got a little soul left. And I'm—I told you—
Having trouble with angels, who shed

Wings like coconuts, who want to remind
Me of your eyes and hands and tongue
And the promise and the anger,

The Ridiculous Human Quotient,
The way we fill our hearts with things
That can speed away

That just bar the way
While all the time I know . . . it's breaking.
And you want to lay your head down and rest—

And I want to taste your breast on my tongue,
Travel the continent, touch
Your hand in the dark, sleep with your breath—

There's only a little opening left
For the light to get through. In the middle
Of this poem, the telephone rings

And the name comes up "unavailable"
So I answer, thinking it's got to be you.
But it's a computer, a prerecorded offer.

This tree's dropping bombs
On me/you. This sheltering/shattering
Of broken things, telephone rings,

Sweltering silence, brief summer.
This old dream undying,
Undying.

His Eyes Are Closed

He's sitting next to me.
It's Thanksgiving.
I have brought my lover home.

Brother-in-law and sister,
Mother, father, lover, and I.
There are no pictures

To document our differences.
In this photo, my dad leans away
As I lean in and hug him.

His eyes are closed; he doesn't see
How far I stretch to sling my arm
Around his shoulders like a boa.

He's laughing, maybe this is why
His eyes are closed. My eyes
Gaze toward the lens,

Although I squint between expressions.
I see his teeth, his open collar,
The camel-colored V-neck sweater

My mother had to give away
Along with many others.
Where are his glasses? I wonder.

No one takes them with him under.
Not many dress down for death
But don a suit and tie.

His eyes are closed. He never saw
This picture—or knew how far I had to reach,
How hard I worked to hold him.

Kennewick Man

Someone found Kennewick Man
Washed up on the shore—
9,000 years of bones.

Bury him or study him—
Two cultures in one can't decide
What needs to be done.

He might be Polynesian,
Not Asian as continental drift suggests.
Either way, the tribes say he belongs.

A white man was found in his house
After only two years. Neighbors
Said he wasn't a friendly guy,

And one day he just disappeared,
Stepped inside from the porch
And dropped dead in his easy chair.

His house was sold for taxes owed.
Neighbors said that no one missed him.
Indians claim their Kennewick man.

The Man in the Basement

The man in the basement
Slips in liquid,
Requests the band play "Yellowbird."

The man in the basement
Flicks a silver lighter
To his Kent.

The man in the basement
Flips a quarter—
Produces a dry mop,

An antiquated adding machine—
Catches the coin
In one hand, turns it over on the other.

The man is down there
With fertilizer, mildewed tuxes,
Cummerbunds, with grass seed

And birdseed, detox,
Electric shock, and bourbon.
Down there inevitably

And forever, his orbit
Is small—size 9 Allen Edmonds—
But persistent, a satellite

Tied to a space station set adrift.
The man in the basement
Inherited a crude wooden box,

A child's coffin
For iron tools too heavy to use.
The charred chest is down there

In the basement
Near the ping-pong table
And the upright piano whose middle C

Has one half of its ivory
Cracked and gone. He is down there
Fox-trotting, making up steps

Beneath a bare bulb,
Writing out chemical recipes
For unguents and agents,

Cures and catalysts, infant
Cough syrups, and homemade bombs.
The man in the basement

Can't be bothered now. Don't
Call him to meals. Don't
Bug the living "H"

Out of him with your questions,
With your longing.
Yours, all yours,

The stone in your chest.
The man in the basement
Cannot break camp.

Shore Leave

My father's glasses washed out with a wave.
Knee-deep in flashes,
A shoal of minnows slinging past his pale legs,

He sank. Time after time his feet
Suctioned off the ocean floor.
Buoyed on a big kahuna, he bobbed out

Beyond his height, beyond the breakers.
We lost sight of him in 1999.
In the necessary dark an image resumes its flicker:

R&R in Hawaii, leis and a slanted grin.
This was before the end, before the winning and
The losing.

Air Walker

Above my head, a spider walks the air.
A shadow falls upon my book.
I turn the page

And look up at the spider, so much
Smaller than its shadow,
Spinning air without a net.

Surely Emily wrote a verse
About this spider's twirling passage
That has stood the test.

A narrow fellow comes to mind,
The buzzing of a fly.
I cannot read what's next.

Subzero Summer

So this must be what it feels like to be dead,
Shivering on the solstice,
Tipping the scales off my eyes,

And seeing the pitons lose their bite. Do
Dead folks party? In Dante's Inferno
At least they have friends.

It's not a good idea to wind up frozen
In a fault of rock. Petrified remains
Get treated to an inquisition.

Even the stomach yields artifacts
To be tenderly charted.
And when they open that last

Little laboratory—which used
To be a cherished part of you—and tweeze
Out your confession, what will you

Tell them? That everyone was wrong,
That your better judgement
Reached one hundred percent,

Making you really god, though no one knew?

Moth to Flame

Burning on my lawn
After a storm,
A young cardinal roots for a worm.

You've got a way with women
Who want to take you home,
And one of them waiting

While you pick up the phone.
It takes a certain stratocumulus
Charge and lack of resistance

For lightning to reach ground.
By the sound of your voice
It's another singeing moth to flame.

The fire's crackling in my bed
Like the line just before it goes dead.

The Goat Falls Ill

Three in a tree
Darken
Possibility.

The clover patch
Conceals
Skull's bright, garnet cap.

Pitched on apex,
Talons
Gaff rusted metal.

Six wings abide.
Poor goat's
Collapse is final.

The What Ifs and If Onlys

A certain pair of married couples
Traveled everywhere together—
If four were ever one, it was these people,

The What Ifs and If Onlys.
You'd never dream of inviting one set
Without the other, and even if you forgot

They'd show up with wine
In hand, as if by your design.
If only you were beautiful

And what if you were bold?
If only you had said the magic words
That transformed sorrow into joy.

What if you had taken the job?
If only he had called.
What if you had crossed the road

A second earlier or later?
If only you had understood, or
Waited or not waited. What if

You had spoken the truth
Instead of obfuscating?
If only you had hedged a bit

And let her think the best. What if
You had been kinder or blinder?
If only you had been born rich,

If only you had gone to Smith.
What if you had taken the train
To Memphis? If only, what if—

Here, allow me to help you with that.
Mr. If Only is such a gentleman,
Always opening doors for the What Ifs.

Ghost Family

A big welcome to the Ghost Family Reunion.
We only meet at funerals
In Holiday Inns south of the Mason-Dixon.

In little-used backwaters,
We blend into the scenic Blue Ridge Mountains
Or follow our progeny to the Atlantic

As if we were a river winding to the coast.
But we are only a few sad reminders
Of the legions on the other side of the line:

Your sister, your husband, your aunt,
Uncle, cousin, mother, your father,
Your brother, your youngest child.

It's just a bad dream when we wake in cold,
Air-conditioned rooms, but our fashions
Confirm it: black stockings and black lapels,

Matched boutonnière, a touch of black humor.
If only this were prom night
And not a dance macabre.

With so many gone now, it's a shock
To have one more burial to attend.
It's like our own service after a while—

We start taking issue with the hymns,
Choosing our favorites, humming them
Instead. We want a jazz funeral, but then

We stop ourselves to wonder if we're still
Alive and kicking. And if we are not, what
Would it take to raise us from the dead?

And if we are still breathing,
What would it take to make us feel something
More than sad? Line us up and shoot

Our formal portrait. We're the Ghost Family
Reunion, the short living in front,
All the dead towering over us to the rear.

Pepper, 1930

A dark puckering means over the hill, off
The vine, misbegotten of time,
Forgotten.

That I am singing in the dark
For direction. That I am locked
In the dark heart of an Edward Weston

Photograph of a green garden pepper,
Nothing exotic. And yet not even
The pepper itself can guard its sensual

Thoughts. They range, reveal, conceal.
When I buy a pepper
I rinse it under tap water. I sometimes

Tap it for steam, scraping
Out the white seeds
As if I could purify us both

And suspend what might happen.
Then I wash my hands, collapse
In a heap, fall down and worship

All nature wrapped in thin green skin, the slick
Curve of an expressionless face,
Everything and everyone who has carried

Us to this place.

for Tig

How to Stop a Camel

The reins feel as insubstantial
As shoestrings slipping
Through the eyes of your hands.

You are riding blind with terror.
The humpbacked beast gallops,
A runaway train, car stalled

On the crossing. Hanging on
To its mane, you reach for one rein
And pull, training the force in a circle.

After the first dread and frothing,
The camel brakes, ever so slightly.
A few more swipes of this compass

Around a shrinking point, pinning
The tail, and your future loops
Your past, shooting out through

The present moment. The animal
Bows as you dismount.
Survival brings its own pleasures.